A Window, a Fence and The Sky Beyond

The poems of,

Mary Winifred Cowhig

A Bootle Girl

a celebration of life, faith and the joy of nature, includes her prayer book for animals

Dave F Cowhig

Copyright © 2025 Dave Cowhig

ISBN: 978-1-918264-70-8

All rights reserved, including the right to reproduce this book, or portions thereof, in any form. No part of this text may be reproduced, transmitted, downloaded, decompiled, reverse engineered, or stored, in any form or introduced into any information storage and retrieval system, in any form or by any means, whether electronic or mechanical, without the express written permission of the author.

Foreword
A Window, A Fence, and The Sky Beyond

Mary Winifred Cowhig described herself as just a Bootle Girl. My first memory of my cousin was as a six-year-old at my grandmother's tiny flat on Scotland Road in Liverpool, in 1956. Sadly, my Aunt Elizabeth terrified me as she wanted me to fetch her false legs, which were warming by the fire. She liked to heat the metal before attaching the legs to her stumps. During the May Blitz of 1941, she didn't go to the air raid shelter; instead, she stayed under the stairs, which local people believed was the safest place. A direct hit collapsed the stairs onto her legs, which had to be amputated at the scene. Mary guided me to stand behind her as she remonstrated with Aunt Elizabeth. I would have nightmares about these legs running after me, but Mary would always rescue me. She was my protector. Mary was eleven at the height of the Blitz. She told me that when the air raid alarm sounded, they would run to the shelter. She would always have her bible with her. As the sound of the bombs fell, everyone in the shelter prayed. Later, the news would be delivered on which street had taken a direct hit and if they knew anyone who lived there. In May 1941, over eight nights, Bootle, Liverpool, became one of the most bombed places in England because of its proximity to the docks. 20,000 people were made homeless, and 1,000 people were killed. Mary lost many school friends.

Soft spoken, caring, with a teasing Liverpool wit. Fiercely proud of her family. She hated injustice long before racial discrimination became a prominent issue; she was an advocate for social justice. Her love of nature is reflected in many of her poems. Her steadfast faith in God is evident in her Prayer Book for Animals, where each creature questions its purpose in God's creation, and in her Christmas prayers.

Mary was born in Bootle on November 16, 1931, and died on December 25, 1997. The last 23 years of her life, she was housebound in her living room, suffering from Multiple Sclerosis. The title of this book is "A Window, A Fence, and The Sky Beyond," which she referenced as her only view of the world.

No longer able to climb the stairs, her bed was placed in the living room, and for 23 years, her devoted sister Lilly slept on a sofa to be close to her, giving comfort and aid throughout the long hours when Mary was in pain. And it's during these moments that Mary found inspiration. to write her poetry. You will hear her conversations with God in her writing as she leans on her faith, finding respite from her suffering.

To the reader, I hope you come to know her and enjoy her story through her poetry, as well as the peace in her conversations with God. Her love of people, nature, and the world inspires all of us. Mary Winifred Cowhig: A Bootle Girl.

Dave F Cowhig

Art and Design by Zac Champian, thank you for all your hard work and Anthony Horn for formatting the cover

Grateful Thanks to all the NHS nursing staff who cared for Mary

Contents	Page
A Child in Church	1
A Circle of Prayer	2
A Garden Revisited	3
A Prayer of Parise	4
A Simple Prayer	5
A Star Bright Night	6
A Thread of Hope	7
A Word for Everything	8
All Things Pass	9
Christmas Greetings 1	10
Christmas Greetings 2	11
Contentment	12
Dawning	13
Evening	14
Everybody Everywhere	15
False Freedom	16
Galloping By	17
Happy Dayes	18
Here to Stay	19
Housebound	20
If Wishes Where Horses	21
It's So Obvious	22

Lost for Words	23
Love is a Sailing Ship	24
Maggie May	25
Marin Luther King	26
Memories	27
Monday	28
Nellies Early Bedtime	29
Noon	30
October Day	31
Ode to a Prune	32
Paint Me A Picture	33
Party People	34
Progress	35
River Dreams	36
Salute to A nurse	37
Seasons of Time	38
Solitude	39
Some Folks	40
Someday	41
Spring Came Softly	42
The Christmas Bus	43
The Depression	44
The Dragons Flame	45

Eternal Promis	46
The Humming days	47
The Moon on The Water	48
The Parting	49
The Raggedy	50
The Rain Laden Breeze	51
The Shroud	52
The Silent Cargo/notes	53/54
The View My Window	55
The Visit	56
The World Spins Around	57
Then and Now	58
Thoughts	59
Time Out	60
To The Few	61
Who Me	62
World Full of Rain	44 63
Yet Another Rainy Day	64
Yours The Tops	65

The Prayers and Poems for Animals

A Dog Called Rip –	67/68
Gypsy	69
The Pryer for the Bever	70
The Pryer for Warthog	71
The Prayer of Cage Bird	72
The Prayer of the Camel	73
The Prayer of Caterpillar	74
The Prayer of the Dolphin	75
The Prayer of The Lion	76
The Prayer of The Otter	77
The Peacock Prayer	78
The Prayer of the Vulture	79
The Prayer of the Whale	80
The Prayer of The Wolf	81
The Meeting or the Waters	82

A Child in Church

Tiptoeing into the waiting church, dark pools of shadow splashing onto a sunlit floor.
Pausing near the heat-flaked door, collecting straying thoughts flying like feathers in a breeze.
Ink-stained fingers dipping into holy water fonts held by angels rapt in meditation.
A calm and cool place after the summer heat, the sound of my sandaled feet whispering up the aisle.
A quick greeting to each solemn-faced statue, and indeed, there's a fleeting smile as candlelight shifts.?
A world at war, and here, a small moment of peace, as a schoolgirl lights a thin candle of hope, its heat curling and rising in supplication to the unseen God.
Row upon row of upright benches, polished and prim, stiff and without comfort to the knees.
Mournful organ music duets with birdsong outside stained glass.
Trees tapping reminders of time passing.
Candle smells and flower smells mixed with lingering incense, fixing in mind an intense and instant reminder for future years to be recalled to comfort, an older but little wiser one, seeing with a clear inner eye an altar cloth lovingly embroidered.
'Will you not watch one hour with me?'

Written this from memory during the May Blitz of 1941, walking to church. The weather was warm with a beautiful blue sky.

A Circle Of Prayer
A circle of prayer to link us all.
To hold us close in a sheltering shawl.
Though far apart from touching hands.
Thoughts are there as linking bands.
A circle of prayer, a good cause to rejoice.
Just heart to heart, it needs not voice.
From city to city and far beyond. . .
Linking kind thoughts by a godly bond.
Ever outward from you. . . you and me. . .
Widening over each shining sea.
Enclosing, encapsulating in moments of prayer.
All grace from God we can all share.
In sorrow and sickness, in each dark day.
God is there to lighten the way.
Candles of hope and circles of prayer. . .
Could lighten corners of God knows where.
So, pray for guidance and peace.
Our circle of prayer need never cease.

A Garden Revisited
The dizzy money spider with promises to pay.
Link crimson-hearted beauties, entrancing heads away.
Shining lines of wonderment on the dusty roads of time,
Back to buttercups and daisies and flaunting dandelion.
When knee high to a marigold, I stood before a rose,
And I knew a wide-eyed sense of joy that reached down to my toes.
I studied all the tiny hearts of buds just newly born,
And wondered how god made them. Was he up before dawn?
I fingered cool blades of grass when summer showers ceased,
And knew a garden was indeed a sumptuous kind of feast.
Candytuft and larkspur and humming of the bee.
Lupins and wallflowers wind tousled peony.
Slanting rays of sunshine dappled on leaf folds.
Tall blue spires of stock the scented memory holds.
There's a fat, furry caterpillar sneaking through the soil.
Assailing heights of hedging to curl in a velvet coil.
The child I knew... the woman knew it too.
Creams and pinks and copper bronze colours of every hue,
Delight the eyes and smooth the mind, made careworn by day.
A garden has the ability to steal the heart away.

A prayer of Praise
God- Creator, Redeemer, Friend
God- My beginning, Being, End
God- Sustain me on my way
God- of the furthest stars and moons
God- of the arid sands and dunes
God- of the smallest specks of dust
God- whose every word I trust
God, please guard my every hour
God- protect me with your power

A Simple Prayer
Give ease to my mind, Lord –
And peace to my heart.
Strengthen me, Lord –
that the tears may not start.
Stretch forth your hand
When my spirit is low.
Let me walk in the path
You want me to go.
Each day, Lord, let me know your will
Each night, Lord, let me be still-
Still to know that you are near
To dispel from my mind-
the last traces of fear.
You carried your cross; help me with mine.
Let me know the love divine.

(This seemed to form itself in my mind when I was feeling low one day)

A Star Bright Night
A star-bright long, long ago.
When the Son of God was born.
A small, stable shelter protected him when his mother was tired and worn.
The cattle lowered the babe to sleep, and the shepherds knelt in awe.
On a night full of wonder, long, long ago, God came to a poor stable.

Angels' choir sing on high.
A song of love and joy.
Shepherds kneel in humble praise at the feet of the newborn boy.
The cattle gather, soft-eyed, still.
So little one can sleep.
His mother, with Joseph standing near-
Tears of gladness weep.

A Thread of Hope
Clinging to a thread of hope.
And spinning, spinning, higher and higher on the thread
of hope and turning, turning.
Will the thread fray and break, and I falling, falling?
Who knows? Who cares?
Enveloped in air-tight anxieties, aimlessly rocking.
Closing doors and gates foolishly locking.
Many moments of unconnected time are lacking.
Who cares? Who knows?
Forests, dark and twisted nights.
Calling, Calling.
Cold winds, ice, borne chipped
Freezing, Freezing.
All alone in loneliness.
Crying, Crying.
Who knows? Who cares?
Who'll bring a light?

Someone said that the sane can't imagine the mind of the insane. I wrote this trying to feel the isolation and despair.

A Word For Everything
'Pass me over the thingamajig'
Before it comes too late.
The car is full of giddy flies, and the whatsits is out of date.
Quickly hand me the oojah.
Just look at what it spilled.
Have you got a miximar? This dingjar must be filled.
There's a suitable word for everything.
What a snazziful world it is.
Unless you're a trifle 'Dumpydown'
And a wash with a 'Grumbelfizz'

All Things Pass
How I'd love to hear my footsteps
Quick. Sure, full of life, walking free once more, but there
they are, silent, stiff, subdued feet.
Not dead but a throb with a devil in each pore.
How I'd love to feel the rain wet upon my face and the sun
upon my skin and smell the shore.
To reach and touch the branches of the trees.
To hear the skylark singing in exultation.
But I hear the squabbling sparrows, and they are a joy
indeed. One who
sees life through a window, sun through glass, I take and
hold the
moment, for all things pass.

Christmas Greetings 1
Hold out the hands of friendship
Hold out the arms of Love
For the child born in Bethlehem
On a night with the stars above
As remembered now on this happy day
Was born in a stable, bare
The King of Kings brought so low
To show us love is near.

Christmas bells ring out, ring out.
Christ the lord is born.
Christmas chorus, sing out, sing out,
In the starry dawn
A virgin mother brought to birth
in a stable small.
Brought God's love to all the earth
And God still loves us all

Christmas Greetings 2
Love shines out at Christmas
Through a child in a stable was born
Love shines forth from Bethlehem
like the sun coming up at dawn,
Those we love and hold safe in our hearts
Our family and friends so dear
These words may be fleeting, like time itself
But love outlasts all the years.

Holy bright hours and paper chain days
Fill your heart with cheer
Know this card brings greetings
At this happiest time of the year
Remember the babe of Bethlehem
Where shepherds came to praise
Smile with Mary, mother of one-
Who colours all of our days

Contentment
I love to pull the curtains wide to see the dawning day.
To watch a lone plane scratch upon the sky with silver wings.
To see the seagulls fly in swirling dizzy circles. Like trippers
torn twixt roundabouts and swings.
And on days less than gloriously fine, when black-sailed pirates
clouds race towards the east.
And the wind whips the privet hedge far out of cultured line.
There too is pleasure on which the seasons feast.
Fire replaces daylight and touches braso aglow.
And purring cat curls upon my knee.
A hand resting lightly on the dog's shining head.
And a book shrouded deep in mystery.

Dawning
Sparrows are spaced on the fence in three-fourths time
Skipping notes of a morning anthem sold on the cheap
A mob of feathered agitators flexing tiny muscles at a bleary-eyed world wishing it was still curled in unthinking sleep
Small bullyboys in noisy dispute, squabbling over petty crime under the eye of a black bird.
Wondering, soft-eyed, at their lack of a good upbringing.
He flies away to sing the song as it should be sung from a caring heart.
A day promising much in rash good humour, believing wild rumours of a fine day ahead.
Clouds racing before the sun's early vigour, swift fading brushstrokes, in a soon lost masterpiece, wind-tossed modern art.
Blurring and clearing in the blink of an eye, changing shape and shade as they run out of town.
The west wind touches the roses, fluttering last season's petals in a brief but merry dance.
Then, moving on so restlessly for new leaves to tease in a moment's entrancement.
A dawn of blue and gold, stolen from the dying summer to October's dazed enchantment.

Evening
Silent- the evening now is silent
and still the hurry flurry of the day
Children called indoors, mutinous and pleading
Then, only the stars are moving
Just the ticking of the clock measuring the quiet minutes
chopping at them the only intrusion.
Nights soundless feet steal away the tired day
and sleep stills the recent whirl of mad confusion.

Everybody Everywhere
Everybody everywhere seeks happiness; it's true.
But finding it and keeping it seem challenging.
Difficult because we think that happiness is found.
Only in the places where wealth and fame abound.
And so we go on searching in palaces of pleasure.
Seeking recognition and monetary treasure.
Unaware that happiness is just a state of mind.
Within the reach of everyone who takes the time to be kind.
For in making others happy, we will be happy too,
For happiness, you give away returns to shine on you.

False Freedom
False Freedom rides with a white horse.
And looks a gallant choice.
Smiling widely in the sunlight.
He makes the heart rejoice.
Fair words to gladly follow.
Running headlong where he leads.
Rallying to a misty banner and talking of fine deeds.
But his face is made of evil.
He hides behind a smiling veil.
He lights a torch of mischief.
To run through Hill and Dale.
So, weigh his words and study.
Where false freedom bids you stay.
All cry hot tears of acid.
Where true freedom lost its way.

Galloping By
So many facts outside my head
So many books yet unread
The world is still unfed
As time goes galloping by
So many songs there for singing
So many bells for ringing, but the doves of peace are not winging
Yet time goes galloping by
Empty swings in a vandalised park
The young take drugs all for a lark
Following each other to the devil's ark
Still, time goes galloping by
People speak words, but nobody hears
The lonely shed their unwiped tears
Blind, time goes galloping by.

Happy Days
Come with me to Daisy Chain Days.
When life was full of fun, Summer walked down winding lanes.
Shadow dappled by the sun.
We shrugged off passing showers, your far-off yo-yo years.
When tears turned swiftly to laughter, and laughter turned swiftly to tears.
Helter-skelter hours running wildly through the days, golden fields of buttercups.
A burst of summer blaze.
The songs we sang were merry ones as we skipped away the hours.
Chasing endless butterflies that dipped among the flowers.
Childhood days of innocence are all too short a time.
Deserves a recollection within the limits of this rhyme.

Here to stay
Why disturb the dust? Dear.
Asked the old man in the chair. I read it in a book, dear, that one over there.
 There are one thousand facts and fancies, but the bit about dust is a fact.
It's flakes of skin and fragments of hair. You might show a little tact!
I'm resting on that sideboard and mantle shelf; all the dust above the rest is
probably your good self.
So, leave me well alone, my love, leave the dust to lie.
For its only you and me, love. I guess we're here to stay.

Housebound

Months come and go, and where go I?
I look up at a grey, hooded sky.
Searching for a thread of hope
Just enough to string my hopes on to.
Children run, and my mind races.
Shaking loose from pain's tight races.
Pills to mark the passing days
While I remember well walked ways.
Days dawn and die; I watch them go.
Night drags its feet, the hours so slow.
Only in dreams can I walk free
Without pain to keep me company.
Why? I ask the answer comes, why not?
I count my blessings and discover quite a lot.
And in the chill dark stillness of the night
I know, I know that God is my light.

If Wishes Were Horses
If wishes were horses, I'd ride like the wind.
Through cloudbanks and valleys and time.
I'd race the fast swallow and head the high hawk.
And when the day was dying, I'd slow down for a walk,
To see the stars beckon and watch the full moon.
If hope were a candle, I'd kindle a thousand and string them all out in the black.
velvet sky . . . and if they all died with the grey skippered dawning . . . I'd light
them again and never ask 'why.'
If time were a river full of sparkling, clear water, flowing onto the fast-changing
sea, I'd trail my hand in the wake of the boat, but it wouldn't slow down just for me.
If prayer were a blossom tree tended with trust throughout life's long-ridden days,
may god, rich in mercy, let it bear fruit before I return to clay.

It's so Obvious
I sat there, thinking deep thoughts
About how to put the world to rights
As I catch a glimpse of my face in the mirror
And wince at the awful sight
Such a dropping mouth and down lizard eyes
And I think, do I look like that
I shrugged off the world to go its own way
And turned to our beautiful cat
How is it, puss? You look so fine
Please tell me your secret, do
As she preens and purrs with a secret smile
And content with the day, aren't you
She smiles again in pity for me
And waved a languid paw
Humans collect worries to add to a pile
And then look around for some more
Now I sit in the sunlight and feel its warmth
This moment is enough for me
And I know in my heart that when people look
They do so admiringly
But, cat, I said softly, that's not fair
You've got a start on the rest of us folks
That's true, she said with a nod of her head
And I find it all quite a joke
That long, long ago, when our lives were in plan
I was born into the world of cats
And poor you to the world of man

Lost for words, Lord
I can't seem to pray, Lord, she whispered, not as I did as a child.
Then I prayed for the world with favour, but now my mind runs wild.
They've closed the local church to keep the vandals out, you see?
But all I know, Lord Jesus, is it's all barred and bolted to me?
Her eyes reddened with memories of tall candles lit in prayer.
Processional white and flowers smells and visits with time to spare.
Lord, I'm so often lost for words; once I was lost in dreams.
I wanted to change the world, but I was the changeling, it seems.
Lord, this isn't the best of offerings. I'm distracted by the crack in the wall.
The whole room needs painting, and there is a damp patch in the hall.
Lord, my mind is full of sidetracks. What happened to Faith's Highway?
When I knew full well my direction, and now, I've just lost my way.
Oh! There's the doorbell now, Lord.
Will you please have patience with me? I will really try and pray later, but I'm so
out of practice, you see. Oh! Lord, you'll know why I'm laughing! My grandson
Martins has just been. He's got a job, "he said," thanks to you, Gran, the greatest prayer expert ever seen.

Love is a Sailing Ship
Love is a sailing ship.
The heart is its harbour home.
Life is ocean-wide on its wild waves we roam.
Dreams fill the soaring sails.
We sail with the morning light.
We follow the sun by day.
We steer by the stars at night.
An old fisherman once sang this song as he mended his nets in the sun.
His father, before him, sang the song to his bride as their long voyage began.
Love is a sailing ship.
Though we be tempest-tossed.
Hope is our figurehead.
Our ship will not be lost.

Maggie May
Dedicated to the Dakota.
Good old Maggie May, it's plain you're here to stay.
Painted, proud and nose up in the sky.
Reflecting on your glory, a great lady in a story
That will never fade away and die.
You and your sister fought a war back in forty-two, sleek, haughty, and brand-new.
Then you fell on woeful days, unhearing songs of praise.
You quietly thought of what had gone before.
When you lived through desperate hours in hostile, cloudy towers.
You gave all your sparkle and your fight.
You're not meant to stand around immobile on the ground; a bird-like you is meant to take flight.
Tomorrow, Maggie May will be loved as yesterday.
Soaring vistas once more flying high, and as you take to wing, the engine voice will sing,
Oh, good, good old, good old Maggie May.

Inspired by the Liverpool Echo report on restoring a veteran Dakota plane. And ships often seem to live, especially to those who fly or sail in them.

Martin Luther King
Martin Luther King is dead.
Death came swiftly- a bullet sped.
Dark night fell, and bright day fled.
Martin Luther King is dead-
Martin Luther King is slain
Nothing can be quite the same again.
He searched for peace and found only pain.
Martin Luther King is slain.

But Martin Luther King lives on
He lives in story
He lives in song
He lives in the hearts of all goodwill.
So, Martin Luther King lives still.

Written 4/4/1968

Memories

All the days of misty mornings- and the dawn of cold white clouds
All the walks of lengthening shadows come to mind and live once more.
All the webs of weary spider's diamond dropped in dew, newly formed.
All the frosted leaves of winter, sharp edges, filed in memories, stored.
All the lacy trees of summer and the speckled thrush's song.
All the cat's paw's seaborn breezes blow again from the western shore.
All the gentle gauze of gleaming deepened to a dark-winged night
With all the friendly stars of childhood, shine again, heavenly core.
All the fog veils on the river and the mellow fields of corn and the
Suntanned children laugh again at memories door.

Monday
Sounds of the morning come unbidden
Sounds of wet-spun street
Hug the night, reject the dawning
Hold fast, dreams that now run fleet
Morning blares and shakes the weary
So little time to bless the night
There's no delaying days' loud call
And eyes open to cold grey light
Out to the hustle and bustle of the battle
Last in the befuddled, huddled queue
Sleepy meddled, cold wind battered
Was there such a motley crew?
Broad-backed worker, lunch in pocket
Queue-jumps with fluid ease
The rain relents and gently ceases
I see the birds in stately trees
Rain-washed roses, pink and glowing
Scent assails the inner heart
Memory captured- stored – safe hidden
Balm for Monday's grey-hued start

Nellie's Early Bedtime
'Nellie, come in, it's time for bed!'
'But mam, the sun's still shining and it's my turn for the rope!'
'Nellie, don't dare start your whining, get inside this instance and up the stairs!'
'But mam, there's no school t'morrer and you know I get the horrors-
'if I sleep too long!'
'Our Nellie! How many times must I tell you? They'll hear me in Hong Kong!'
'But mam, everyone else stops out, you never pick on our Jackie-
'but I'm treated like a lackey. The sun is still shining; I've just got the rope!'
'I've raised my voice here,' my hand's there, partners! Get in and up to bed.'
So Nellie returns the skipping rope, and a young face dark in sorrow, she mutters, 'Flippen Heck'
Reluctantly and truculently, she climbs the stairs to bed.
Now in a tone soft and cooing Nellie starts booing!
Mum calls sweetly in a tone so honeyed,'
'But mam, the sun's still shining -me and Joe'n 'n Eddie are nowhere nearly ready-
'and it's my turn on the bike.'
'Alright son, another half hour and if it starts to shower- come and get yer mac!'

(Wrote this because nobody ever seems to call children to bed as they did years ago- no two-tone yelling- all the children pleading for 'Five minutes more!')

Noon

Noon-High temple of the day
The pulsing, searing heat.
The frowning, thirsting time.
When the clock fingers meet
No softening shadows-no scarves of mist
No velvet flowers, new dew-kissed
The sun is king, and everything must bow
The cruel death of morning
On the sharp apex of the day.
High sun and low spirit- tattered nerves affray
No curving caresses to gentle the trees for the weary, no soothing balm.
A furnace blasts a trumpet call.
Move on Time to the evening's quiet charm.

October day
Gold, bright sky of welcome warmth
Stretching wide, the morning light
Dawn takes breath. Day comes anew
To startle black and chilly night
The trees ' leaves of dying brown
To cover cold and sullen stone
Gold turns to pink and moves to cream
As days blue clock is skyward throne
The autumn morning fills with song
As day advances through the sky
Birds leave the nest to test the air
And joyous raise unfolds and fly
Then rises man from square cocoon
To blight the day with search and smell
And turn sweet haven into hell.
With ponderous feet, he treads the ground
Blind to beauty all around.
Metal-armed, he rides the road.
And fills the air with hooting horns
Mindless machines drowned the day
It dies unknown, unloved, unmoaned
 Returned at dusk to the plastic-flowered flat
On nights cold heels, he stomps the welcome mat
And shuts out the icy splendour of the stars.

I thought this up on the 95-bus going to the English Electric factory when I saw the most beautiful, spectacular sunrise. No one noticed the splendour; they were all reading the papers or sunk in glume. I felt like shouting, "Hay, look what's happening!"!!

Ode to a Prune
O little frizzled, wizened face
Do you know your proper place?
You and all your company are very close to me.
Dark of feature, dark of deed
Yet I follow where you lead
To see you nestle on my plate
Fills me with both love and hate
For I know that you'll not bide
And that you'll take me for a ride
This fleeting meeting cannot be.
For you and I part company
So, prune, are you friend or foe?
I must confess, I do not know
But I'll leave some room for doubt
Be sure your sin will find you out.

Paint Me A Picture
Paint me a picture of shimmering sands.
Rocky faced cliffs, stark as nature had planned.
Cottonwool clouds on a blue linen sky.
Paint me a picture to gladden the eye.
Paint me a picture of children at play,
Dressed in colours to vie with the day.
A baby asleep: A wide-eyed young fold.
Paint me a picture to gladden the soul.
A picture of fresh, wide meadowlands.
The variant fields like green ribbon bands.
A snowy-backed swan: A seagull in flight.
Paint me a picture to make the heart light.
A picture of sparkling, sunlit streams.
Mountain heads lost in the fine mist of dreams.
A copper beech tree: A garden in flower.
Paint me a picture to gladden the hour.
A picture of ships home from the storm.
Slippers by the fire, welcoming and warm.
A faithful dog: A kitten with string.
These are the things to make the heart sing.

Party People
So glad you could come, though green-lidded eyes say otherwise.
White teeth bare and flash in compound lies and light-fingered handshakes
Limp and pass quickly as March showers go around the circle of shining fools.
Glitter on sparkle, glimmer on gold, and here, where no one ever grows old in friendship deep, Rancour rules.
Where, remember, it goes no further back than the day before yesterday? It is because there is no real commitment or attachment to the swift ships of the night that pass in sleep-clouded hours.
Send no flowers for the death of false friendships. . . all eyes and teeth. . . and no pulsing heart, destined to part.... like breath from the mortal body of frail Mayfly. . . born to die.

Progress

Go – progress must proceed; no need to intercede.
Just pack your life and go!
Begone – so the motor car can speed and like a monster feed
on lives and hopes and dreams!
People are expendable – you didn't know?
You thought you had your place- a place you called your own.
Fools – build your castles in the air.
Build them anywhere – but don't leave them here
Where the faceless, sightless ones sweep away the past.
For you, the die is cast. Just pack your bags and go- at last.
We're the builders of tomorrow- and if it causes sorrow.
Well, go!

(Two elderly women are being evicted to make way for a new motorway. Held out by living in the attic)

River Dreams

Misty vails on the Mersey trail across to home.
The busy, bossy ferry boats whirling wakes of foam.
Ghost voices whisper softly yet clearly beyond belief of
long sunny hours spent on golden sands.
Building tall sandcastles with small, freckled hands.
Sand grit-filled sandwiches ate in children's haste
Linger in my memory with their very special taste.
Long gone hours, long gone days of laughter, games, and fun.
Paddling and searching all the sunlit pools.
Then, all too soon, time for home when feet dug in like mules.
Aw, Ma'am. . .Aw, Dad, just another half hour...
But pleas and tears unheeded.
We'd gather the litter, board the busy ferry, and watch the lights flitter in homes across the way.
We'd gather all our thoughts together to save for another day.

Salute to a ten out of ten nurse
Oh, nurse Pitt, 'tis pitiful, you leaving us
But being very British, we won't make a fuss.
We'll grit our teeth, stifle sobs, and bravely smile.
Wave our little hankies . . . singing all the while.
'Good luck, Good Health, God bless you.'
May lick stick to you like glue.
Whare ere you go, where ere you be.
You're welcome for a cup of tea.
Come to us when you see fit.
You are to us the Epitome of wit
Nurses are paid a pittance and are angels, it's true.
Though we're unlikely to know ANGELS?
Margaret... we know you!

Twice a week for five years, Nurse Margreat cared for me along with all the other nurses. I will never forget them. God Bless.

Seasons of Time
Spring, a sunny ring of daffodils
Dancing in drifting dreams or mad and fluttered things
Spring a lightness of step and hope in the heart, a fresh new start
A time to sing
Summer-rich fruits, a burning glow, slow growth in long sunny hours
Soil and seedlings intertwined to reward the aching toil, many flowers
Butterflies trapped in a sunbeam.
Summer a sweet taste on the lips, sun in the eyes
Singing birds in limitless skies, a time to dream
Autumn bronze and golden, but sad, as a dying rose is sad, fading red and fading pink
A stately processional pace, moving in allotted time
And measured space, a slowing down,
A watering place, a time to think
Winter, a white shrouded wonder, knife-sharp air
Start studded skies, full moon blessed
Frost-reddened noses, open fires and singing kettles
Christmas cribs and red holly berries, and a time to rest

Solitude

Solitude, a quiet pool of thought
God's gift to the burdened
A gentle heaven's rest
Solitude a ticking of the clock
The contented purr of the cat
The absence of intrusion
Solitude, for some, a blessing
For others, an iron-clad prison
Accused loneliness
Solitude, time to think, to weigh the hours
To measure the minutes of the day and drowse in the firelight glow.

Some Folks
Some folks carry clouds like brides carry flowers
Some folks moan all day and tearstain all the hours
Some folks are tissue-thin and crumple in the rain
Some folks trust in God's good time. The sun will shine again.

Someday

Someday, I'll go to Piza before the tower falls.
Someday, my heart will listen when Paris calls.
Someday, Rome will beckon golden in the sun.
I'll gather my dreams together and run.
Sometime, moon-silvered the Taj Mahal, I'll see.
Sometimes, I'll watch the sun slip down to a tropical sea.
Sometimes, I'll see the ancient Valley of the Kings.
Sometime, I'll hear the lullaby a Fijian mother sing.
Not today or tomorrow, but some time is coming soon.
I'll visit Venice and Rangoon, Snowcapped Mount Fuji –
New York's dizzy heights, Niagara's mighty waterfall-
Sydney harbour lights – and if I never
travel the highways of the world- and only see English
green and pleasant land unfurled?
What, then, will I be missing if 'someday' is never seen?
The dreams that are most cherished are the dreams of the untouched scene.

Spring Came Softly
The winter sunshine told its lies; it fooled me once before.
But now, at last, comes Spring's sweet song through a quarter-opened door.
A gentle song to warm my icebound heart
A rising song to lift long-buried hopes
A song to make the new buds dance and twirl dizzy, spellbound praise
And lead this winter-weary one into summer's golden, mellow, hazy
The eternal promise, once more, is kept
Spring came softly while I slept.

The Christmas Bus
Waves of words, eddies of laughter.
Parcels, holly and sprigs of mistletoe.
Voices mingling, 'Hope this fits him'-
A Michelin man, that's my Joe.'
My poor feet, I'd love a cuppa.
Got a shirt for Ken—and a scarf for Kieth.
Sit down, Carol, you are a fidget –
And tell Les to get back to his seat.
Wipe your nose; Jimmy Santa is coming.
He's trying to find you a big book on sports.
Watching the bustling, giggling children.
An old woman sits – an island of thought,
The young mother's eyes meet the old lady's eyes. I'd like
to sell my kids for a quid.
You're lucky – you don't have the bother,
The old woman nods, wishing she did.
She thinks of her lonely, echoing flat.
Cards cherished through all the long years.
Thinks of the loved ones gone far away –
And blinks back an unseasonal tear.

The Depression

Monday morning – on top of the world
Full of zest and brim-full of health,
I felt euphoric, so I started to sing.
Then came the depression by stealth,
Sickening for something? She said with a frown.
You really look quite frail. Have you got a fever?
There's a sheen on your brow.
I gave a loud inward wail.
Cousin Flo she died, went off the same way,
She'd go all cold and then hot – Lost your voice as well?
It's the self-same virus you've got.
Do you know your eyes are all red?
Maybe that's conjunctivitis,
Why have you started twitching?
Do you suffer attacks of St Vitus?
Months go by – I'm really under the weather,
Flu hangs about like the folds of a hood,
I meet the Depression – how does she greet me?
Well, I've never seen You Look So Good!

The Dragon Flame
Why on earth do you do it?
You have youth and health.
Why chase the Dragon
In secrecy stealth
Do you do it for kicks
To be young is a high
Yet you trade in your future
I'm left wondering why?
Future what future
Is that what you say
There'll be no tomorrows if you take drugs today
So why chase the Dragon down a foolish road to death
For the Dragon will kill you, you'll die in its breath

The Eternal Promise
Concealed in ice veils, stand trees like marble formed.
Cold-fingered arms outstretched before the winter wind.
Shadows of the summer sun forgotten.
Songs of Summer forgotten.
Songs of summer birds are unheard.
Winter clasped fainthearted yet somewhere stirring a promise of spring.
Not yet, not soon, but spring will return.
To lift to warm, to light, to colour, to issue new life into being.
So, stay in winter, stay if you want, stay if you must.
While I take an eternal promise on trust.

The Humming Days
In the humming days of summer –
When the swallows head for home.
Bees buzz from flower to flower
To fill the honeycomb.
Cloudlets. White and golden,
Angel's cushions in the sky.
Days to breathe the sweet summer air.
And softly sigh.
Bless all the flush abundance.
Of summer now unfurled.
God's gracious gifts to cheer the burdened, overweary world.

The Moon on the Water
Follow the moon on the water
Pale golden carpet of dreams
Shimmering shadows of the day that has gone
Black, fringing the dancing moon beams
Silver flutes echo from dark distance hills
Floating the notes through the air
Questioning calling from nights long ago
Before the world knew so much care
When the young world waited and hoped without words for a day to be born pure and free, A day without evil or malice or woe, the world waiting still restlessly

The Parting
She stood rambling, minded, steering into the overly
bright morning, and vaguely wondered why.
It rained from a blue, cloudless sky, then, feeling her face
with trembling hands.
Realising tears spilt like salt from a seller and know a
moment of contentment.
Tide by a silken tether
He had gone, the cruel system had swallowed him, but she
would wait for his return, reviling all the springtime
happiness they had known together.
Hand in hand, seeking the far side of the hill
Unmindful of the swift passing years until
And now the sharp pain would not stand still
She felt a singular kind of fool
Today, her small and only son
Had started infant school.

The Raggedy Doll

Only a poor old raggedy doll with twisted legs askew,
Her faded dress, torn and limp, minus a black cotton blouse.
Tangled wool, her rain-damp hair, and her sewn-on smile were worn thin.
Someone loved the rag doll once, but now she awaits the bin.
Childish words in a darkened room, her cuddled body held tight.
Whisperers into her vacant ears dispelled the ghosts of the night
A dismal end on a dismal day for a raggedy doll so worn.
Now she flops, dejected and sad.
Poor raggedy doll, all forlorn.

The Rain-Laden Breeze

Charmingly gentle, the rain-laden breeze.
Trifling rifling a girl's shapely knees.
Tugging, touching her lowly hem to heighten the interest in watching men.
Tiresomely teasing, the rain-laden breeze.
Snatching, catching, clutching at trees.
Pulling, culling their new leaf green, then moving and leaving a might-have-been.
Bullying, brutal, the rain-laden breeze.
Damningly whirling with sure expertise, a girl holding her hair in place, trying to keep her coltish grace.
Blindingly irksome, the rain-laden breeze.
Amusing itself like a swarm of bees.
Stinging the patience of all the tossed, twisting and towing, not counting the cost.
Then, it grows in strength. The rain-laden breeze, tiring of playing, puts on a squeeze, raising its voice to a curdling wail and leaving behind a fearsome trail.
It's done with pretence and winsome ruse, toying with trees, a full-throated gale with nothing to lose.
It's a storm, a landed gale, and people bow before its progress, they cravenly cow.
There's a warning to all to find the lee.
God help those who sail the sea.

The Shroud
The Shroud that speaks through silent centuries
The witness of the risen lord and we who hear the voices of ages listen, speechless and overawed.
The story is told of the pain and torment of the man who died for all.
The clear, brutal time exposure speaks to us as a clarion call.
They face majestic, noble suffering.
The body is marked by lashes and nails.
Forgive us, lord, our part in history.
Have Marcy, lord; we're weak and frail. We need the link to the living Lord.
Our minds in darkness need enlightening.
The Easters from which grace is poured.
The message the shroud conveys, from heart to heart, is a word sublime.
Tells of love, all other love transcending
A love without the chains of time.

The Silent Cargo

A sorry, silent cargo- a bleak horror
Story told in cold black print, the all-conceited folly of men
Stark photographs of speaking eyes telling of a sick bewilderment,
delivered from the skies, unwanted, not knowing the why of it all.
Created and carted in a cruel commission.
Left simmering in the heat of the Italian sun, until stout hearts fail
and bright eyes dim in doleful death, while soulless bureaucrats
fuss and flounder in a useless, flurried search for tissue authority.
Who is to authorise God's creatures to stay or go on the haughty say-so
Of flimsy papers? Man's belated permit to pass his punny frontiers.
Papers can't breathe- or run in the summer sun, or drink from limpid pools
or smell the sweet, sweet grass
The lie is gathering quiet dust in sullen files given but brief credence by self-important fools and oafs.
Until the animals, released and at final peace, poor wretched waifs of late
are far beyond man's heavy-handed ministering.
Unwilling stakes in a sordid game of chance.
Unwelcome wallflowers at a time-consuming dance of death.

*(wrote this because of red tape causing the deaths of
Zebras, Antelopes, and elk
When a plane was held up for six days at Rome airport,
'Necessary Documents'
Not provided- out of 49, only 16 are alive. The survivors
went to Bahrain?)*

The View From My Window
Slate grey as a pauper's misery
Seagulls, white as purity itself
Bricks red as a summer sunset
Sparrows, brown as old Mother Earth
Privets green as springtime gown
Sky blue as a butcher's apron and scarlet as a martyr's blood
Crimson as a cardinal's robe
Pink as a baby's velvet cheek and yellow as the bonny buttercups in the fields of youth. The view from my window.

The Visit

Kissing cousins, long unseen, visit us with smiling eyes.
Outstretched hands span the years, ties once more the drifting ties.
Soon, the room buzzes, saying, 'Do you remember when?'
Good heavens, that was fifty-four. Eddie's Lad was only ten.
Slyly, I sneak out a hand to click a microphone alive.
All foolish planners should be deported. What happened to the Lime Street dive?
Catch the chatter: Catch the laughter as merry whirls go dancing past.
Hold the memories: Keep the moments: Sure, and safely now, tape cast.
Old jokes retold: Old songs re-sung. . . Adaline is still so sweet.
Then, Boson, our sole singing dog, gets to his four prancing feet.
Cheers. . . applause. . .Maggie May sang loudly, Gypsy our cat retires to rest. . .
Smirk. . . This will be good, Self-satisfied Pat. But, alas, woe is me: the dratted battery is quite, quite flat.

The World Spins Around.
Sunshine - or showers
Minutes – or hours
Weeds – or flowers
The World spins around.
Waking – or sleeping.
Laughing – or weeping,
Giving – or keeping.
The world spins around.
Sense - or Nonsense.
Sound – or Silence.
Peace – or Violence.
The World Spins Around.
Smiles – or Sighs.
Truth – or Lies.
We live – or we die.
But the world spins around.

Then and Now
Once, I saw scenes in the fire
The fires of my childhood years.
Once, I saw cities and castles of gold.
Now I see only my tears.
Once, I saw green waves dancing with sunlight, each one partnering with each one.
Now green waves are grey, reflecting the day.
The sunlight has dwindled and gone.
Once I saw snowflakes falling, and my child's heart would fill with delight.
Now, when I see snowflakes falling, I think how cold night grows.
I'd hear the wind whistling through the summertime trees.
I'd sing along with the tune.
But summer leaves fall, and now the wild wind is howling grief to the moon.

Thoughts
Thoughts of my childhood years.
Of warmly golden days.
Of gazing at star-filled skies
When the moon was pale, sliced melon
Thoughts of long-gone hours.
Of Autumn walks of dogs long dead.
Of snowball fights with laughing friends
When the moon was unattainable
Thoughts of leaping flames of yesteryear.
With magic caverns deep inside
Wherein lurked dragons breathing fire
And rockers belong to November
Thoughts of queues four deep, yards long.
For films seen from the 'one and nines' which thrilled or chilled or laugh-filled, and space was the great unknown.

Time Out
Let me sleep and journey into the foot-free land where wild and golden stretch the mind.
Lively, I dance and speak in grand and uncontrolled way, the big finish to a day of small beginnings.
No tight movements or rained-in words, but swan-like grace and singing praises.
Merry laughter fills in the blank spaces that form when dreams subside.
Pillow soft and sheet cool, a time for myself as I would wish to be.
Swift and slight like a leaf on the tide, riding through a world of timeless joy.
Darkness diminished by heroic light -gone on a whirl of vapour,
and I walk a sunlit road without shadows.
Without thought for tomorrow's basket of woes.

(Mary made a footnote that it should be read like a Shakespeare piece.)

To The Few

Forty years ago, when Britain stood alone.
The shadow of a madman upon his blackly thrown.
The throbbing of a mighty fleet rent the bright sky.
And young men found the time had come to fight
and angry die.
'Scramble-scramble-scramble' off they went to war.
A few young eagles soaring, the clouds became their floor.
Apprentice lads and college boys, librarians and clerks.
Defending mother country with guns, fast spitting sparks.
Some fell like dying, Icarus, plunging from the sun.
Others lived to fight again when this battle had been won.
Turning dulling spirals in the theatre of the sky.
And losses fell to yawning earth; a scream became a sigh.
They fought for the land that gave them birth and won
with
their lives a small plot of earth.
The shining coin of youth was spent, like ugly, worthless
dross.
A gallant few carried a Nation's far too heavy cross.
Brought freedom to this good land of ours.
Their history written among the timeless stars.
Forty years on survivor's viewer still.
At the fountain of fame, they drink their rightful fill.

Written 1980

'Who Me'

Count my blessings – who me? I haven't any'
And she stood and gave the lie.
'Count blessings?' What can I count?'
She gave a deep and mournful sigh.
'Blessings, you touched my funny bone.'
'Well, I've enjoyed our chat and the meal, but
now I must go home – did I tell you we're off on holiday?
me Joe and I and the kids, all rush and expense. Life's not worth living
sometimes. Life is one big fence!
Then off she walked, passing the quiet, sleeping cemetery, and the pain-filled
hospital wards. Passing Oxfam posters and an NSPCC van.
'Blessings? Huh!' Not seeing the blind man near her holding out his thin, seeking hand.
She walked by the grey walls of a mental home, she in the pink of good health.
Still, she did not count her blessings, despite having an untold wealth.

World Full Of Rain 1944
We stand in a world full of rain
And wait for an overdue train
The train that will take you
And the thought seems to burn
If you leave now, you will never return
you smile, so I try to smile, too
Once, you said I should always wear blue
Blue's my colour. It blends with the day
The train will soon come, and you'll go on your way
You speak, but your voice is a sound
Soon lost in the clamour around
A child is crying, or could it be me
I look for the train, but my eyes cannot see
The train comes like a swift afterthought
I cling to the flowers you brought
A last kiss, then you're boarding the train
And I'm alone in a world full of rain

Yet Another Rainy Day
Rain-hushed streets washed new, clean
Hedges weeping over garden walls
A chin-in-hands day of muted sounds
Like far-rushing waterfalls
A sleeping, yawning day, somnolent and drowsing
The sky a flat dullness, like pewter on a dark corner shelf
A dripping, drooping day, sighing for a bright tomorrow.
Raindrops falling headlong down the windowpanes like a fond family funeral.
Tears of sorrow.
Heavy and swiftly paced, one on another raced – again, again, more rain.

You're the Tops
You're the tops. You're the Radio tower.
You're the tops, how you fill the hour.
You're the Philharmonic—your two Cathedrals Tall.
You're a liquid tonic- I'm not laconic, so I'll tell it all.
You're the tops- you're the Pire Head landing.
When you pull out stops, you leave others standing.
You're the Liver Birds- (Now, what's the word?) You've Nouse.
Your St George's Plateau. An Ice cream gateau, a plate of scouse.
You're a tune - the whole Kop choir.
You're so high – you're an Aintree flyer.
Ten years have passed – you're the pick of all the crops.
So, in case you ever doubt, you're the tops.

(This is about Liverpool)

Animal poems and prayers

A dog called Rip

We walked through the seasons of many a year, a dog named Rip and I.

His coat the colour of the autumn leaves

His tail forever held high

Springtime walks on dancing feet

The once stark trees now green

We ran with carefree joy of spring to the great distant scene.

Summer came to daisy-strewn fields

We walked in the afternoon

Life was a long leafy lane

But summer ends too soon

Rip walked with a new and jaunty step as autumn

quickened its pace

The brown leaves fell with a sigh for the past. The wind took the place of the soft breezes.

Then came merry-hearted Rip, the season of delight.

He plunged in the deepest snow drifts.

He caught snowballs in flight.

From bossy pup to faithful dog.

A gentle-minded friend

Till life's long, rich story came to the last chapter's end.

(Rip was thirteen when he died. A great fun and wonderful friend. A cross corgi- I said to one old lady – and she said 'he shouldn't be allowed out if he's cross!)

Gypsy

Small black cat with golden eyes

that follows the flight of the butterflies.

Small velvet ears twitch fitfully

as they catch the drone of the bumblebee.

Turn to the sky, black satin nose to capture

the scent of a crimson rose.

Long bushy tail that twists and turns with

a life of its own in the long sunlight beams.

'Ah, ' said the cat, 'this life is bliss', and accept

from the sun, another kiss.

The Prayer for The Bever

One moment, Lord, I must put this in its place: there it is, done!

It is I, the beaver, who speaks to you.

I have struggled to build this dam; now it is ready to stand fast against the rushing waters,

Is it not good to see, lord, the sturdy results of all my labour? Industry is good, lord.

And now, for the moment, I can rest. I heard it said that you were a woodworker.

And in my small way, I am proud of that; I am also a worker after your fashioning.

Many marvel at my tenacity, and I, in turn, marvel at others' indolence. Still, Lord, you know what you are about.

I cannot idle any longer, delving into things beyond my understanding. I have much work to do.

Aman

The Prayer for the Warthog

Lord, were you tired when you created me?

I'm not exactly one of your best efforts, am I?

With a face only a mother could love.

If my future depended on my looks, I would be extinct.

But I scratch around for consolation and find my steely character worthy of note.

Indeed, I am courageous, certainly tenacious, certainly unwavering in attack,

Unswervingly loyal to my offspring.

Lord, I have thought anew of my ugliness and concluded good looks are for butterflies of this world.

The pretty trivialities of life.

Thank you, Lord. I look as I am- INVINCIBLE.

The Prayer of the Cage Bird

Lord, I swung on my perch, I watched the drab sparrows fly into your limitless blue, and my happy chatter comes from an empty heart.

I look into the oval mirror that sits next to me; I am indeed wearing a coat of many colours, but Lord, am I all dressed up and yet have nowhere to go?

I would give my brightness away, could I but be free to soar away to the heart of the sky- yet I remain- it's hard to say

AMEN

The Prayer of The Camel

Lord, I am the camel 'Ship of the Desert'

Why is man an acquisitive creature?

Foraging here, there and yonder to add to my burden?

Sometimes I feel nothing in the world has rested on my back.

I look at man with contempt; I spit out my disappointment.

Fool! He cannot see what is as plain as the nose on my face; life's essentials are

lightsome things. Why carry all the items of long-dead civilisations?

The lumber of fripperies hangs heavy.

Ah! The caravan has rested now, I must move as I am bidden.

Thank you for my strong back, direct my steps and lord – protect me from straws

Aman

The Prayer of the Caterpillar

Lord, can you see me? I'm the humble caterpillar.

I hug your brown earth faithfully and lovingly.

You had your reasons for creating me.

I fit somewhere into your grand scheme of things.

Though it's hard for some to accept my right to exist.

They have their sprays to support their case.

I can't run from there, fatal minds, what will be, will be.

Yet sometimes I have a hazy dream, no longer a poor earthbound creature.

I dip and flutter among the flowers.

It is so wonderful; is it a foretaste of paradise?

I do not deserve it, but I look upward as I climb with great anticipation,

Soon, lord, soon.

Amen

The Prayer of the Dolphin

Lord, here is the dolphin to speak to you and thank you for the cool depths of your oceans after the warmth of your sun.

Thank you for my agility in racing ahead of the ships.

Carrying my cousin, the man, I like to keep him company, home safely to port.

I look out for him when he is in difficulty; his ability to survive the dangers is beyond my capacity.

He is not always grateful to his guardians, but then he is not always grateful to his creator.

Some seek to destroy us because we, too, are fishers.

They talk of their livelihood as though we are expendable; they destroy so easily, but can they create?

Lord, you know all the answers; we just know all the questions.

To return to the beginning, thank you for the sun and the beautiful sea.

Amen

The Prayer of the Lion

Lord you have made me king, the king of all beasts, many run in fear from my voice, even the tall trees tremble as my displeasure echoes in the green darkness of your jungle, my muscles ripple under the gold of my coat and my great heart beats noble as I stride my domain, but you are great, lord, greater even than I, and I who bow my head to one- I nevertheless bow humbly to you who gave me this cloak of majesty. Strong as I am, Lord, I know you have allotted my reign; give me my strength that I may never abdicate in weakness, old and feeble. No, Lord, as befits a KING, make my passing swift and clean, that when I fall, none may pity.

Aman

.

The Prayer of the Otter

Lord, here is the Otter. See how I can dive and plunge!

See how I can twist in sparkling circles, and the waters thrash and foam.

See my unbounded energy! I have made a long, muddy slide on the steep riverbank.

And wheeeee, thank you for all my happy fun.

Lord, it is easy for the unthinking to compare me with the industrious beaver, but lord, I am me.

Utterly indebted to you for making me an Otter.

My antics give a lift to burned hearts. Do I excuse myself too much?

Perhaps so,

Lord, but I ask for little-

Fish when my family need it and long, frolicsome hours to please my impish heart.

I hope sometimes I make you smile!

Thank you, lord – Wheeeeeee and Amen

The Prayer of the Peacock

Lord, it is I. The Peacock people say I am proud, but I want to set the record quite straight, as I think it is a matter of interest. You understand?

They look at my strutting walk. And fountains of glory, tail feathers, my high-crowned head. And say again, with no knowledge at all, I am proud.

Could you please give mankind the insight to see that in admiring me, glorious creature that I undoubtedly am, they glory you, creator of all my magnificent splendour?

Colour their drab lives with just a little of my spread of shimmering tints, just a little of my bright appeal, but leave me my eye-catching tail so that I may impress my humble spouse.

Amen

The Prayer of the Vulture

Lord, I am the vulture, evil of countenance, evil of deed, or so man would portray me with a poor understanding of my role in life.

I study man my detractor, and find him guilty of far greater misdeeds than I.

I keep your world sweet and unpolluted by scavenging the fallen. Who would

want to live in squalor? Without my good officers, your world would be

unclean. I am necessary to an orderly world. I expect no thanks, Lord, but

would you direct man to examine a conscience here, a motive there and leave

me to wait patiently in my harmless huddle.

Amen

The Prayer Of the Whale

Lord, I am the whale. Hunted as I am, I ask for shelter. Your world is a puzzlement to me. Man sends my hunting song through space to the stars yet seeks to kill the singer. There are times, Lord, when I wish I were as small as the sprat, instead of the massive creature that I am. You decide I must breathe the air above my security – the hidden depths- and man lies in wait for me to surface, as I must. Lord, I sigh for the peace to sing my song in a sea forever blue, unstained by the brief, bright redness of my lifeblood. Send man on other errands and make me a clock of invisibility to hide my great bulk. Protect me from the harpoon and let me rest a while, in peace with you.

Amen

The Prayer of the Wolf

Lord, I am the wolf, vilified in song and story. I'm distressed by it all. I seek only my freedom and the ability to hunt through your vast wilderness. In legend, I am a beast to be feared and, without mercy, hunted and destroyed. What have I done to deserve such a fate? Those who judge me from a great distance know nothing of my love of family, faithfulness and regard for my fellow wolf. My reputation is shredded by you, man, people who give my good name to one who lightly flirts, but my mate is mine for life. I am not without heart. I tread an honest path. They look through telescopic sights and see only a target for destruction. Show me the way through all dangers to my lair.

Thank you, Lord.

Amen

The Meeting of the Waters

There is not in the wide a valley so sweet

As that vale in whose bosom the bright waters meet

Oh, the last rays of feeling and life must depart

Ere the bloom of that valley shall fade from my heart

Yet it was not that nature had shed o'er the scene

Her purest of crystal and brightest of green

T'was not the soft magic of streamlit or lit

Oh no, it was something more exquisite still

www.ingramcontent.com/pod-product-compliance
Lightning Source LLC
Chambersburg PA
CBHW052109070526
44584CB00017B/2411